Getting
Started
with your
Pendulum

**A Tool to Access and Verify
Intuitive Information**

By Mary Baxter

© 2009

Table of Contents

What is Pendulum Dowsing?

The pendulum is a tool used to access intuitive information, that is, information that is not conveyed to us through our physical senses. Pendulum dowsing is just one method of dowsing. Sticks, rods, and L-rods are other tools used by dowsers for geomancy, the science of locating energy fields in the earth – most commonly water. You may be familiar with the use of dowsing rods to determine good locations for water wells.

Another form of dowsing, requiring no tools, is muscle testing, or applied kinesiology. In muscle testing, there is the two-person method, where the extended arm of one individual is tested for strength or weakness, and the hand method, which one person does by herself, using both hands.

In all these methods, there is the connection to information contained in a field of energy that is not available through our physical senses. In other words, we can't see it with our eyes, hear it with our ears, feel it on our skin, smell it with our nose, or taste it with our tongue. Yet, we know it is there.

Now, consider that each of your physical senses has an intuitive component. This intuitive aspect for sight is referred to as clairvoyance or clear sight; for hearing, clairaudience or clear hearing; for feeling, clairsentience, and so forth. For example, in cases of after-death communication, a person may experience hearing a particular piece of music, or experience smelling a particular scent associated with the loved one who has passed on, yet there is no physical source for the sound or scent at the time it is experienced. In these cases, the intuitive aspect of the senses is stimulated, and it conveys the presence of the one who has transitioned.

The Human Energy System

When using a pendulum, we are making use of the human energy system, specifically the electrical system. There are electrical currents that run along certain channels in the body, the energy meridian system well documented in Chinese Medicine, and used in acupuncture, acupressure, massage, etc. This electrical system is a key to connecting with information beyond our physical senses. I'll show you how when we get to the training of your pendulum.

Intuition

Of course, using a pendulum is not the only way to connect to our intuition. We are receiving intuitive messages all the time. This is your connection to what you might call your Higher Self or Soul. Spirit guides, Angelic Beings, your Guardian Angel, or loved ones who have transitioned from their Earth incarnations are among other sources of intuitive information. And even if you do not believe in these ideas or beings, don't worry. You likely have a sense that there is wisdom within you. That is all you need. If you think you have no inner wisdom, try this out. Then, you will discover it.

What is an intuitive message?

Intuitive messages come to us in the form of certain feelings, particular thoughts, even through dreams and hunches. Paying attention to our intuition is often discouraged in favor of what is called "rational thinking." Rational thinking means paying attention only to what is physical, really to what can be replicated in a science lab. Unfortunately, this overlooks a tremendous amount of our very real human experiences. It is a great idea to use *both* our rational and intuitive minds in our daily lives.

Our physical bodies are equipped to provide us with intuitive information. We all absolutely have a sixth sense that works with our physical senses. We get 'gut feelings' that let us know if a situation is comfortable for us. We are told to listen to our hearts to know the truth about a person or situation.

In fact, scientific research done by the HeartMath Institute found that the heart has its own *actual brain* that receives information *before* the brain in our head, sparking intuitive knowing that immediately precedes rational knowing.

In the early 1900s quantum physicists discovered the Zero Point Field, theorizing that there is a universal vibratory field that permeates everything. This field is assumed to be filled with waves and particles that are frequencies containing information. These waves and particles function non-locally: they do not obey laws of time and space. Using intuition, we can access this field with awareness at any time, and in any place. This field is always interacting with us, as it permeates the physical. Some call this the Akashic Record.

A question I have asked myself is why would anyone want to deny the existence of intuition? Or, why would anyone not want me to develop and pay attention to my intuition? These are interesting questions. I encourage everyone to develop her intuition. It encourages independent thinking, self-trust, and increases your potential to live the life you are born to lead. It can also save a lot of time and money.

Bio-feedback Tools

So, where does the pendulum fit in? We don't *need* the pendulum to pay attention to our intuition. However, it is a fantastic tool to open you up, expand your understanding of what your intuition has to offer, and provides a very accurate tool for really honing into the information that is available beyond our physical sensory experience.

I first discovered the pendulum when I decided to learn to read the Akashic Records – a vast spiritual library containing all the information of everything that has ever happened everywhere, throughout infinite time and space – a library some think may be physically embodied by the Zero Point Field of Quantum Physics.

As you become experienced with the pendulum, you will find your intuition blossoming. You may be surprised to find you are clairvoyant or clairaudient, although you were not before.

Selecting Your Pendulum

At its most basic, a pendulum is a weight that swings freely on the end of a string, a plumb bob. So, you can experiment with pendulum dowsing quite easily. Yet there is something very personal and special about finding a pendulum that is just right for you. As I design and make the pendulums in my collection, each is a sculptural jewelry piece that adds to the beauty of pendulum dowsing.

Choosing the pendulum that is right for you is a very personal matter. I have had all kinds of pendulums. When I first began using the pendulum, I chose one made of glass, cone shaped, with a silver chain attached to the wide round end, the point facing down. I liked the idea of glass, thinking that it was a clear substance that did not have a signature matrix of energy, like a gemstone. I was thinking about clarity. When I lost that one, I chose a brass pendulum. This was heavy, a round ball with a brass chain coming out of the top, and the round ball curving into a point facing down. I kept losing pendulums. Honestly, I think my cats made off with them to play. I went on to using faceted Austrian crystal baubles, small faceted ones that were very light and made beautiful dancing patterns in candlelight. I began to make simple pendulums by stringing a strand of silk cord through a 10 or 12-millimeter frosted quartz bead. This way I knew I would never be without a pendulum.

Now, I enjoy the creative process of designing and making pendulums with glass, gemstones, spheres and other shapes, and 14 Karat gold-fill. From my years of pendulum dowsing, working with gemstone energy, and all forms of fiber, my pendulums are little sculptures that I have a great time making.

You may find your pendulum in a metaphysical shop or at an intuitive fair you enjoy visiting. The most important thing about choosing your own pendulum is that you are drawn to it. It speaks to you, calls out to you, makes you want to hold it and have it and use it. Perhaps you will even begin to make them, too.

Cleansing Your Pendulum

You will want to wash your pendulum, whatever it is made of, in warm soapy water to physically clean it before you begin to use it. Next, it is important to cleanse the energy that is attached to it. There are several ways to go about this.

You can burn sage and let the smoke touch the pendulum. You can cover it with sea salt, a very cleansing substance that resonates with the D# tone, which is also the tone of sage. It is a tone that neutralizes negative or disruptive energy.

Here is the energy cleansing ritual I like to use with a new pendulum: Take a large square of fabric, like a white or purple scarf. I like silk. Lay it on a clean surface and place your new pendulum in the center. Take the sea salt and form a closed circle around the pendulum. You could light a white candle, or do this in bright sunlight. Cupping your hands, with the palms facing downward, directing energy toward the pendulum, give your blessing to your new pendulum. For example, you might call on God, the Four Directions, or the Great Goddesses. I say the following:

Creator of All Beings (x3)
Please place a blessing on this pendulum,
and tone it to the D# tone, giving it a Creator Truth Ray,
that it may be used in love, and light, and truth,
in the highest good of all.
Thank you. (x3)

Feel the blessing and cleansing energy flowing through you, into the crown of your head and out through your palms and then into your pendulum. Your palms may feel warm or tingly. As the feeling subsides, circle your palms in a clockwise direction three times. Pick up your pendulum, gaze at it, and bring it to your heart. Then bring it up to the center of your forehead. Now it feels more a part of you.

Training Your Pendulum

When someone sees a person using a pendulum, it may look like the pendulum itself is being spoken to - as in, ask the pendulum. I don't think of it this way at all. We are not talking to pendulums, and having pendulums answer us. The pendulum is a *tool*. We train our electrical system, which is a key intuitive pathway, to move the pendulum in ways we choose, so that we can read the messages being conveyed through our intuition.

How to Hold Your Pendulum

I use my right hand to hold the pendulum. This is my dominant hand, the hand that I write with. I feel awkward whenever I try to use my left hand to dowse. The movement of the pendulum feels odd, unclear for me, much like when I try to write with my left hand. Even now, as I am writing this, word processing into my computer, as I focus attention on my left hand with this description, it feels awkward.

I had thought that it would be very efficient to dowse with my left hand while simultaneously writing with my right hand, but this just hasn't worked out at all for me, although I have seen it work for others. However, I encourage you to experiment with both hands, and choose whichever one feels best for you.

Hand and Arm Position

Rest your elbow on the table in front of you, or the arm of a chair, so that your arm is relaxed and comfortable, your wrist is relaxed, and the cord of your pendulum is lightly grasped between your thumb, index, and/or middle fingers. Again, find what is comfortable for you. You should have a sense of relaxation throughout your entire arm all the way through to your finger tips, without being so relaxed that the pendulum slips from your grasp and falls onto the table. Do NOT dowse with the pendulum over your other hand, or your body. This will distort the responses and lead to confusion.

You can use the following graphic to train the movement of your pendulum.

Yes
clockwise circle

Say, "This is a 'yes', and *make* the pendulum move in a strong clockwise circle, about 3 - 4 inches in diameter.

No
counter clockwise circle

↺

Then say, "This is a 'no', and make the pendulum move in a counter clockwise circle.

Yes
with *more*
questions needed

↗

Make the pendulum move in an elliptical clockwise direction.

No
with *more*
questions needed

Make the pendulum move in an elliptical counter clockwise direction.

Start over
with a more precise question

Then, make the pendulum swing back and forth, horizontally, and say, "This means 'start over'.

Neutral

Make the pendulum swing up and down, vertically, and say, "This is neutral, 'yes *and* no'. When you get these movements while dowsing, it helps you to intuit further questions to refine your ability to access the information you are seeking.

Practice this, moving the pendulum in these patterns several times, to make sure that the training is well ingrained. Then, move on to the next step, which is to stop making the pendulum move, and let your electrical system respond.

Holding the pendulum in the relaxed way described earlier, say, "Show me a yes." The pendulum will move in a clockwise circle, about 4 inches in diameter, just as you have trained your electrical system. Continue with "Show me a no." "Show me a 'yes' with the need for more questions," and so on.

Trouble Shooting

What if your pendulum doesn't move, or the movement is very slight? Don't worry. There is a learning curve involved here, and it deals mostly with your own confidence. You may need to train your electrical system with the pendulum more than once – even each time you want to ask a question – in the beginning. Do not give up. That's the only way it will not work for you. Before you know it, any initial frustration will give way to confidence in your dowsing.

The ways I am showing you are the ways I have instructed my energy system to respond with the pendulum. For some people, a horizontal, back and forth swing is preferred for 'yes', and a vertical, up and down swing is preferred for 'no'. This is fine. This doesn't matter. It is what *you choose*, and the consistency of using it that way, that is the key to your success. There is no reason for a person who already uses a pendulum to change the way they read their messages.

Remember, once trained, you **do not** 'make' the pendulum move. You hold your pendulum in a relaxed position, ask questions, and through your electrical system, the pendulum will move all on its own, to convey the answers coming to you through your intuitive connection.

Connecting to Your Intuitive Intelligence

Who Are You Talking to?

Connect with your inner wisdom, your higher self.

Before you ask any questions, it is *essential,* and I cannot emphasize this enough, that you state your intention through your thought and word, to connect to your positive inner wisdom or your Highest Self, and only to that information which is in the highest good for your life and the lives of others.

What is called the Universal Energy Field, Zero Point Field, Akashic Field, or the Akashic Record, is an infinite library of information containing *everything* that has ever happened, in all dimensions of existence, since the Big Bang. There is a record of you, your Soul, from the moment you separated from the consciousness of the Source, right up to this very moment, including every thought, word, and action throughout every incarnation and between!

This totality of information is completely inclusive, meaning that both truths and falsehoods are recorded. If you do not state your intention to access only information that is true and in your highest good, and simply open yourself to any and all information out there, you may well open yourself to a great deal of disruption and negativity, unintentionally. So, state your intention to connect to truth and light. You can think this. You don't have to say anything out loud, unless you want to.

Here's how I do it. I say:

Let the Creator Light emerge.
May it grow and expand.
I ask my guides and teachers to be present,
and for Truth and Accuracy to be obtained,
in the highest good of all.
Thank you.

You will connect with your inner wisdom, your Soul, perhaps one of your Guides, or another Angelic Being that works with you in this way. I connect through an Angelic Guide who has been with me all of my life. I had always been aware of her, and 'heard' her give me very special guidance at key moments in my life. When I began to use the pendulum, she stepped right in, clearly happy to be given this more direct and frequent communication tool to use with me. Over the years that I have used the pendulum, I have become much closer to her, 'seeing' her, learning her name, and knowing she is always with me.

Asking Clear Questions

To begin, ask some very clear and simple questions, ones that you know the answers to. This way, you can be sure that the training of the pendulum movement is accurate and reliable. For example:

> Is my name Mary?
> Is my mother's name Anne?
> Is my brother's hair blond?
> Am I forty years old?

If you aren't getting the correct answers, keep working on it. It will come together quite quickly as you relax into it and release the impulse to control the pendulum's movement, or suspecting you are when you are not.

You also want to ask questions that clearly have a 'yes' or 'no' answer. Say you have a complex question, such as "Is it most correct that we order pizza or Chinese food for dinner?" Break it down.

> "We can order pizza or Chinese food.
> Which will we enjoy more? Pizza? (yes or no).
> Chinese? (yes or no).

Do you see what I mean? You will quickly learn to ask very precise and clear questions. You will know you are asking clear questions when the answers you receive don't confuse you.

Ideas to Get You Started

Dowsing lists is an extremely effective and efficient way to use the pendulum. For example, make a list of the tasks you plan to do today, in the order you would like to do them, or that seems logical to you. Here's an example of a list of mine:

> Pick up my glasses.
> Write chapter 4.
> Go to the bank.
> Pick up library books.
> Grocery shopping.

Dowse your list, asking, "Which task is it most correct to do first?" (Note this is *not* a 'yes or no' question.) Then, point to each item on the list, consecutively, until you get a 'yes'. Then, "Which task is most correct to do second?" pointing to the remaining items on the list, until you get a 'yes,' and so forth, until you have the order for everything. It may not be the same as what you wrote down in the first place.

Then, go ahead and do your tasks in the order that you dowsed, and see how things go - or follow your original order, and see what happens. With this particular situation, I remember wanting to pick up my glasses *before* doing anything else, because I was eager to try out my new prescription before writing, going to the library, and so forth.

My dowsing indicated getting my glasses later in the day. This annoyed me, so I went over to the optometrist's at 9 AM anyway to pick them up. They were supposed to be available the previous afternoon, but I was unable to get to the office before it closed. When I arrived at 9 AM, it turned out that they had not been delivered the previous afternoon, and I was instructed to return after 3 PM, following the next delivery.

This was a great intuitive lesson, without being huge or life threatening. So, start slowly, and build confidence in your pendulum dowsing through practical daily applications.

Another important point: When we are very emotionally involved in a situation, and heavily invested in a desire for a specific outcome, it is unlikely that we will be neutral, or objective enough, to receive a clear intuitive answer. Our strong desires definitely can impede receiving accurate intuitive information. Keep this in mind. In such emotionally charged circumstances, it is better to have someone else, who has no vested interest in the situation, dowse for you.

Developing Confidence in Your Skills

You may find pendulum dowsing an immediate success for you and a very natural extension of your openness to intuitive information. Or, it may take you days, weeks, a few months or even a year to feel you truly trust the answers you receive. As you practice, you will arrive at a point where you just *know* that you can trust yourself.

Once you have developed your confidence, the entire Cosmos of information is available to you. You will only be limited by your choice of questions. Each of us needs access to our intuition, now, more than ever. I hope you will enjoy the beauty and practicality of this wonderful tool.

About the Author

Dr. Mary Baxter is a teacher and intuitive consultant, helping clients and students worldwide to understand their lives, life purpose, relationships and more. While completing her doctorate in Transformative Studies at the California Institute of Integral Studies in San Francisco, Dr. Mary founded Akashic University, an online school where she teaches the language of intuition and how to actually do research in the Akashic Records. She lives and works by the ocean in Half Moon Bay, CA.

Made in the USA
Middletown, DE
17 July 2021